LIVEWIRE
YOUTH FICTION

All or Nothing

Iris Howden

Published in association with
The Basic Skills Agency

Hodder & Stoughton

A MEMBER OF THE HODDER

Acknowledgements
Illustrations: Maureen Carter.
Cover: Maureen Carter.

Order queries: please contact Bookpoint Ltd, 39 Milton Park, Abingdon, Oxon
OX14 4TD. Telephone: (44) 01235 400414, Fax: (44) 01235 400454. Lines are
open from 9.00–6.00, Monday to Saturday, with a 24 hour message answering
service. Email address: orders@bookpoint.co.uk

British Library Cataloguing in Publication Data
A catalogue record for this title is available from The British Library

ISBN 0 340 72091 3

First published 1998
Impression number   10 9 8 7 6 5 4 3
Year   2003 2002 2001 2000 1999

Typeset by Fakenham Photosetting Ltd, Fakenham, Norfolk.
Printed in Great Britain for Hodder & Stoughton Educational, a division of
Hodder Headline Plc, 338 Euston Road, London NW1 3BH by Athenaeum Press
Ltd, Gateshead, Tyne & Wear.

All or Nothing

Contents

1

A Row at Breakfast

It was Sunday. Always a boring day.

I went downstairs.

Mum and Dad were in the kitchen
eating their breakfast.

'Morning Katy,' Mum said. 'Sleep well?'

'You're late,' Dad said.

'It's Sunday,' I said,

'what is there to get up for?

Where's Claire?'

'She stopped over at Debbie's,' Mum said.

'She rang late. After you'd gone to bed.

She said the demo went well.'

'Oh it's alright for my sister to stop out,'

I said. 'She's 17 after all.

Claire can do what she likes.

She can go on Animal Rights demos.'

'Don't start,' my dad said.

'I want to enjoy my breakfast.'

I looked at his plate.
It was piled with bacon, sausage and egg.
It looked disgusting.

'Yuck,' I said. 'I don't know how
you can eat that stuff. Did you know
mother pigs have to give birth
in a stall so narrow they can't turn over?
So they won't lie on the piglets.
They might squash them.
Lose the farmer some profit.'
'Really,' my dad said. 'How interesting.'

You can't put him off his food.
He mopped up some bacon fat
with his bread.

I tried again.
My mum was having a boiled egg.

'Think of those poor

little battery hens,' I said.

'Kept in cages, so small they can't move

except to eat. They get stressed.

Then they start to peck out their feathers.'

'That's terrible,' Mum said.

'It's a good job these are free range eggs.

Now, what do you want for breakfast?'

I got the box of cornflakes.

and shook some into my bowl.

A little toy fell out.

It was a plastic dinosaur.

'This is you,' I told my dad,

waving it under his nose.

'A dinosaur. They died out.

Like we will – because we're killing the planet.'

'Will you be quiet,' my dad shouted.

'You can go on till you're blue in the face,
but you are not going on any demos,
you're too young. And that's that.
I'm going to read the paper, Anne,'
he told my mother. 'In peace and quiet.'

'Really Katy, you don't go about things
in the right way,' my mum said.
'What's the point of winding your dad up?
He won't change his mind.
He's stubborn – just like you.'
She started to load the dish washer.
'Your dad works hard, and it's all for us.
We have a nice home, a good car, holidays . . .'
'A nice home!' I mocked.
'That's quite enough, Katy,' mum said.
When she uses that tone of voice I know
I've gone too far.
'Now clear up that mess you've made.'

2

A Boring Day

I knew it would be a boring day.

Mum and Dad went out to lunch.

Some friends had asked them over.

I could have gone.

That would have been mega boring,

so I stayed at home. I didn't mind –

I had Max for company.

Max is my cat. He's a sleek tabby with

a purr like a chain saw.

I love him to bits – I love all animals.

I prefer them to people really.

That's why I was so keen to join

the Animal Rights group.

Claire got into it first,

through Paul, her boyfriend.

She wasn't keen to take me.

I suppose she didn't want her kid sister

tagging along.

'You're too young,' she said. 'Only 14.

Wait till you're older, 16 at least.'

It was Paul who talked her round.

'What's the harm?' he asked,

'if Katy makes a few posters and so on.

We need all the help we can get.'

I was pleased. I like Paul.

It's a good job there are people like him.

People who care. After all,
animals can't speak up for themselves.
Someone has to look out for them.

My mum's a kind person,
but she doesn't understand.
'There are so many people in the world,
who need help,' she'll say.
'Hungry children, old and sick people,
I'd rather help them.'

I don't see it that way.
Animals don't have any choice.
People ill-treat them, make them suffer.
Take farming. I don't eat meat,
but I don't mind if other people do.
So long as they treat animals right.
Give them room to move,
air to breathe, grass to run on.

As for testing things on them –
that's the limit.
Putting stuff in rabbits' eyes,
or giving mice cancer.
It doesn't bear thinking about.

I looked at the clock. It was 3.30.
Claire should be home soon.
I went along to her room.
I checked to see if she had any new CDs.
I didn't dare touch her diary. She'd kill me.
Her room was very tidy – not like mine.
It's bigger than mine.
Claire always does best.

There were some ANIMAL RIGHTS posters
on the wall. Nothing too bloody,
just baby seals looking cute.

I picked up the photo of Paul and Claire

that was beside her bed.

Paul's the best looking boy in the 6th form.

Claire's very pretty too, like mum.

She's tall and slim with fair hair.

I'm more like dad –

chunky, with mousy brown hair.

Life's just not fair.

I heard a car door slam outside.

I put the photo back quickly

and made for the door.

I was just in time.

Claire passed me on the stairs.

'I hope you haven't been in my room,'

she said. 'Messing with my things.'

'How was the demo?' I asked.

'Great. I'll tell you later.

I must have a shower and change.'

3

A Row at Dinner

We sat down to dinner.

'How was the demo,' my mum asked.

'Great!' Claire said. 'There was a big crowd.

300 at least. Some stars came from

that animal show on TV to speak.'

'What was it about this time?' my dad asked.

'Transport of live animals again?

People have to eat you know.

Farmers have to make a living.'

'No,' Claire said. 'Not this time.

It was a protest about the new lab.

The one that's due to open in Feltham.

They're going to breed animals –

rats, mice, maybe monkeys –

to use in their experiments.'

'Drugs have to be tested,' Dad said,

'before you can give them to people.'

'No they don't,' I shouted,

'you don't have to hurt animals ...'

My mum gave me a look that said 'shut up.'

At that moment the phone rang.

Dad went to answer it.

When he came back he said,

'That was Jeff Reed on the phone.'

Jeff Reed was a police chief.

Dad knew him from the golf club.

'He says he saw you, Claire
at the demo with that boy.'
Dad always called Paul 'that boy.'

'What's the problem?' Claire asked.
'It was all very peaceful.
We had permission from the police.'
'It might have been peaceful today,'
my dad said,
'But Jeff says there could have been trouble.
He says there were trouble makers
in the crowd. Rough types, hippies.'

I nearly choked on my peas.
My dad thinks anyone who doesn't
wear a suit and tie is a hippy.
'People don't wear their best clothes
to go on a demo,' I said.

'Well,' Dad went on, 'Jeff says some
of these are hard cases.

They'll stop at nothing.

Claire could have got hurt.'

'Rubbish!' Claire said loudly.

We all stared at her.

It wasn't like Claire to argue with Dad.

She went red. Then she said more quietly,

'A lot of the people were middle aged.

The vicar was there from St Marks,

and those old ladies from the cat shelter . . .'

'Well, I'm just warning you,' Dad said.

'Don't get mixed up with anything that's

against the law.

You've got your exams next summer.

I want you to do well at A level.'

I could see we were in for a long speech.

I said goodnight and went to bed.

Next morning Claire told Mum
we'd be late home from school.
'Paul's mum invited us to tea,' she said.
'Katy as well? That's nice,' Mum said.
'Yes, she's helping me with a project.'
It was the first time I'd heard Claire
tell a lie.

'What was all that project stuff?'
I asked as we walked to school.
I'm not too keen on extra school work.
'There's a meeting of the group
at Paul's tonight,' Claire said.
'I thought it best not to let Mum know.'

That's how Claire scores.
She knows how to avoid trouble.

4

A Noisy Meeting

Paul's house was a big, old one.

The gate was hanging off,

the garden was a mess.

Inside wasn't much better.

Mrs Grant wasn't what

you'd call house-proud.

She didn't make us any tea.

'Help yourselves,' she told Paul.

'There's some beans in the cupboard.'

I could see the Grants were into good causes.

There were posters on the walls.

HELP THE HOMELESS,

SAVE THE WHALE,

NO MORE MOTORWAYS and so on.

They seemed to be keen on re-cycling too.

There was rubbish everywhere –

Stacks of newspapers, bottles and tins.

Mrs Grant teaches at the junior school.

She seemed rather bossy.

Paul's dad was a quiet man.

He's a nurse at the local hospital.

He was on nights so he left for work.

The meeting was due to start at seven.

As well as the usual crowd,

there were some new people.

These must be the 'hippies' my dad spoke about.

He would have hated them on sight.

I had to admit they looked a bit strange.

Lads with torn jeans.

Some with way-out hair styles,

studs in their noses, tattoos, and so on.

The girls wore combat trousers and heavy boots.

One girl with bright red hair called Lizzie

got quite worked up.

'If we're going to do any good,

we've got to make an impact,' she shouted.

'It's no good standing about with posters.

It's time to stop talking and get into action.

There's a meet of the Feltham hunt next week.

Let's have a big show of strength then.

Turn out in force. Cause a bit of aggro.'

I saw Claire nudge Paul.

She didn't look too pleased.

'I'll help you make the coffee,' she said.

I went with them into the kitchen.

Claire filled the kettle.

'I don't like the sound of this,' she began,

'I thought we wanted a peaceful protest.'

Paul pushed her up against the sink.

He kissed her gently on the lips.

'Trust me,' he said, 'I won't let things

get out of hand.'

'What do you know about this new mob?'

'Not much,' Paul said, 'but they want to help.

The more people we can get, the better.

We want to improve life for all animals,

don't we?

I know how much you hate fox hunting.'

Claire nodded but I could tell by her face

she wasn't happy. She didn't like

the way things were going.

5

The Hunt

On the day of the hunt we didn't tell Mum
where we were going.
We just said we were going on a bike ride.
This was no lie. We had to cycle five miles
to where the meet was being held.

There were crowds of people.

Lots had come just for the day out.

They brought their children to see the hunt

gather on the village green.

It was quite a picture – a real country scene,

like something off a calendar.

Horses jogged past – lovely animals,

their coats shiny as conkers.

Then the hounds came,

a great pack of tan and white dogs,

their pink tongues hanging out.

Their tails waved in the air like flags.

You could tell they were pleased to be

out for the day.

I was quite enjoying it myself.

Until I thought about the fox.

Poor animal, being chased all day.

How scared it must be.

Then caught by the pack of hounds,

to die a horrible death –

torn to pieces by dogs.

Claire and I stood with our friends.

We held up our posters as the hunt passed.

SAY NO TO CRUEL SPORTS mine said.

BAN FOX HUNTING! said Claire's.

The huntsmen in red jackets swept past,

pushing the hounds on.

They took no notice of us.

'SHAME SHAME SHAME' we chanted.

A man in a tweed coat waved his whip.

'Get this rabble out of the way,' he shouted.

Rows of policemen stood about,

in case of trouble.

The hunt moved on, through a narrow gate.

There was a loud bang – then chaos.

I was too far away to see what was happening.

I could hear people shouting, horses neighing.

Then the police near us began to run.

They ran towards the noise,

pushing us out of the way.

We saw some of Lizzie's mob

being chased from the field.

Claire and I ran towards the gate.

Horses were running free.

Some without their riders.

As we got into the field Paul met us.

He put his arms round us both

and held our faces to his chest.

He led us to the group's van.

'Don't look!' he said.

'Someone threw fireworks.

One of the horses has been hurt.'

He was too late.

We had already seen the horse.

It was lying on the ground nearby.

A blanket lay over it.

The blanket was soaked with blood.

Claire began to cry.

Tears rolled down her cheeks.

'That's it,' she told Paul when he dropped us where we'd left our bikes.

'I don't want to go on with this.

This is not helping animals.'

'You're upset,' Paul said.

'I'll sort it out. Sleep on it.

You can't give up now.

The Feltham lab opens in three weeks' time.'

6

The Raid

The next day was awful.

Pictures of the hunt were splashed

over the Sunday papers.

There was a clear one of us

holding our posters up.

My dad hit the roof – of course.

'How could you get mixed up with

a stunt like this,' he yelled.

'After all I told you not to go.

I do business with these people.

Sir Frank Forbes, the Master of the Hunt

is one of our best customers.'

He went on and on and on.

Mum tried to calm him down.

I think she was afraid he'd have

a heart attack.

'The girls have learned their lesson, Bill,'

she said. 'Let it drop now.'

Claire looked terrible. She went around

looking pale and ill, like a zombie.

She wouldn't answer the phone.

She wouldn't speak to Paul.

'I'm still on your side,' I told him.

'You weren't to blame for that idiot

throwing bangers. Our work has to go on.

Claire will come round, you'll see.'

But she didn't.

'I'm starting to agree with Dad.

We're wasting our time,' she told Paul.

'You know I don't hold with violence.'

'That was a mistake,' Paul pleaded.

'That hot head won't be back.

The police have charged him.'

'I'll still go out with you,' Claire told him.

'But I won't be coming to any more

Animal Rights meetings.'

'It's not that simple,' Paul said.

'We are what we believe in.

You can't just accept part of me –

It's all or nothing.'

'That's it then,' Claire said, 'it's over.'

She didn't go on the raid.

I was surprised Paul went ahead with it,

but he was trying to prove a point.

'There'll be no violence,' he stressed
at the next meeting of the group.
'No aggro, no trouble.
We just move in, as planned.
We'll spray paint some slogans,
STOP ANIMAL TESTING,
NO GAIN THROUGH ANIMALS' PAIN etc,
then move off as quickly as possible.
They won't be expecting a night raid.
They'll expect a demo on the day
the lab opens. We'll surprise them.'

But he was wrong.
We were the ones who got the surprise.
There was quite a welcome party
waiting for us that night.
I'd sneaked out after everyone
at home was asleep.
I wasn't going to let Paul down.

I wore my dark anorak.

I pulled the hood over my face,

and got into the van without Paul seeing me.

I hid in the middle of the group.

It was pitch dark. No-one spoke.

As we drew near the lab one of the lads

pulled some wire cutters out of his pocket.

He snipped a hole in the fence.

We all crawled through into the grounds.

'Fan out,' Paul said,

'some of you go round the back.'

I took out my can of bright red paint.

I aimed it at the wall outside the lab.

Suddenly, all the lights went on.

Men ran out from the building.

Police cars came screaming up the drive.

'There's been a tip-off,' someone shouted.

In the dark it was hard to see who anyone was.
I could tell Lizzie by her red hair.
She and her pals were laying into people
with baseball bats.

The police put a stop to that.
They rounded up her little gang
and pushed them into a van.

I ducked under a copper's arm
and ran to where Paul lay.
A big bloke was kneeling on his chest.
'Get off him, you big bully,' I shouted.
He looked round. Paul took his chance.
He hit him in the face.
I don't remember anything else.
Something large and heavy
landed on my head.
I went out like a light.

7

A Hospital Visit

I woke up in hospital.

My mum and dad were sitting by my side.

There were a lot of flowers

on the locker by my bed.

I think I said 'Where am I?'

– like they do in films.

'Don't try to talk,' Mum said.

'You've had a nasty blow to the head.

You had to have stitches in it.'

'Thank God, you're alright,' my dad said.

He looked really worried.

I knew I wasn't in trouble – for now.

'Where's Claire,' I asked. 'What happened?'

'Claire's at school,' Mum said.

'She'll be along later.

You could have been killed.

One of those young thugs pulled up

a fence post. He meant to hit a policeman,

and got you instead.'

I lay back and closed my eyes.

My skull felt like it had been

bashed with a hammer.

'Get some rest,' Mum said.

'We'll see you later.'

My next visitor was Claire.

She brought me a bag of wine gums,

a mag I liked and some tapes.

I was starting to enjoy being ill.

Claire's eyes were red with crying.

'How are things at home?' I asked.

'How do you think?' she said.

'I got the blame for leading you

into the Animal Rights thing.'

'And Paul? How's Paul,' I asked.

'I've no idea,' Claire said.

'I don't care if I never see him again.

He sent you this by the way.'

She tossed an envelope on the bed.

I opened it after she'd gone.

It was a get well card with a cat

on the front. A bit like Max.

Inside Paul had written:

KEEP UP THE GOOD WORK KATY

ALL THE BEST FROM PAUL.

I had to stay in hospital a whole week.

I couldn't wait to see Paul again,

to thank him for my card.

But I couldn't.

No-one told me he was in prison.

8

A Prison Visit

'We didn't want to upset you,' Mum said,
'not while you were in hospital.
Paul's being held on remand.
His case comes up next month.
The lawyer thinks he's got a good chance
of getting off lightly – if he's sensible.
His headmaster's willing to speak for him.
He's never been in trouble before.
If he keeps quiet in court, says he's sorry,
he may be OK.

But he's like you, Katy.

It's all or nothing with Paul.

I'd hate to see him go to prison.

I like Paul. I admire him for sticking

to what he believes in.'

'Would you tell him that?' I asked.

'Maybe we could change his mind.

We could go and see him –

It's worth a try.'

I kept on at her until she agreed.

'I don't believe I'm doing this,' Mum said.

She parked outside an ugly grey building.

There was a high mesh fence around it.

Rain fell on us as we read the name:

MOORSIDE Y.O.I., it said.

It looked very bleak.

Mum handed a pass to the man on the gate.

We joined a queue.

Soon we were moving into a large room.

It was set out with tables and chairs.

People looked round for their loved ones.

I spotted Paul. He waved us over.

He seemed pleased to see us.

'How are you?' I said. 'I love the outfit.'

He was wearing faded jeans, a tatty jumper.

Paul smiled. 'What did you expect? –

a suit with arrows on it?'

'I've brought you some cakes,' Mum said.

It was my turn to smile. Only my mum

could take fairy cakes to a prison.

'They're not made with

any animal produce?' Paul asked.

I knew he wouldn't eat them if they were.

That's how strong minded he is.

'No. Katy's been teaching me how to shop,'
Mum said, 'I read all the labels now.
I buy meat raised without cruelty and
shampoo that's not tested on animals.'
'Good for you. It's a start,' Paul said.
'Thanks for bringing Katy to see me.'
'Oh, I didn't just bring Katy,' Mum said.
'I know how you feel about animals.
But I want you to hear me out.'

It was quite a speech.
Mum told Paul not to waste his chances.
She told him to go on to University.
Get a job where his voice could be heard.
'You could do more for animals that way.
You'd have real power,' Mum said.
'A lot more people would listen to you.'
I don't know if Paul took notice.
But what Mum said made a lot of sense.

43

Suddenly, she didn't seem just a housewife.

More a person in her own right.

We've all got on better since the raid.

Even my dad can discuss things

without flying off the handle.

Paul gave me a hug as we left.

'Thanks for standing by me, Katy.

You've been a real friend,' he said.

I don't kid myself.

He'll never look at me the way

he used to look at Claire.

But being called a real friend

is better than nothing.